BIG PICTURE  SPORTS

Meet the
SEATTLE
SEAHAWKS

BY
ZACK BURGESS

NORWOODHOUSE PRESS

CHICAGO, ILLINOIS

NORWOOD HOUSE PRESS

P.O. Box 316598 • Chicago, Illinois 60631
For more information about Norwood House Press please visit our website at
www.norwoodhousepress.com or call 866-565-2900.

Photo Credits:
All photos courtesy of Associated Press, except for the following: Black Book Archives (6, 18, 22, 23), Topps, Inc. (10 both), McDonald's Corp. (11 top), Fleer Corp. (11 middle), The Upper Deck Co. (11 bottom).

Cover Photo: Kathy Willens/Associated Press

The football memorabilia photographed for this book is part of the authors' collection. The collectibles used for artistic background purposes in this series were manufactured by many different card companies— including Bowman, Donruss, Fleer, Leaf, O-Pee-Chee, Pacific, Panini America, Philadelphia Chewing Gum, Pinnacle, Pro Line, Pro Set, Score, Topps, and Upper Deck—as well as several food brands, including Crane's, Hostess, Kellogg's, McDonald's and Post.

Designer: Ron Jaffe
Series Editors: Mike Kennedy and Mark Stewart
Project Management: Black Book Partners, LLC.
Editorial Production: Lisa Walsh

LIBRARY OF CONGRESS CATALOGING-IN-PUBLICATION DATA
Names: Burgess, Zack.
Title: Meet the Seattle Seahawks / by Zack Burgess.
Description: Chicago, Illinois : Norwood House Press, [2016] | Series: Big picture sports | Includes bibliographical references and index. | Audience: Grade: K to Grade 3.
Identifiers: LCCN 2015025443| ISBN 9781599537481 (Library Edition : alk. paper) | ISBN 9781603578516 (eBook)
Subjects: LCSH: Seattle Seahawks (Football team)--Miscellanea--Juvenile literature.
Classification: LCC GV956.S4 B87 2015 | DDC 796.332/6409797772--dc23
LC record available at http://lccn.loc.gov/2015025443

288N—072016
Manufactured in the United States of America in North Mankato, Minnesota

CONTENTS

Call Me a Seahawk 5

Time Machine 6

Best Seat in the House 9

Shoe Box 10

The Big Picture 12

True or False? 14

Go Seahawks, Go! 17

On the Map 18

Home and Away 20

We Won! 22

Record Book 23

Football Words 24

Index 24

About the Author 24

Words in **bold type** are defined on page 24.

The Seahawks are fierce defenders.

CALL ME A SEAHAWK

The Seattle Seahawks are named for different birds that hunt on the water. Seahawks use speed and surprise to catch their prey. They fiercely defend their territory. The Seahawks play this way every time they take the field.

TIME MACHINE

The Seahawks joined the National Football League (NFL) in 1976. They were an exciting team from the start. In 2005, the Seahawks played in the Super Bowl for the first time. Russell Wilson and **Marshawn Lynch** led them to their first championship, in 2013.

Russell Wilson raises the Super Bowl trophy.

7

Fans can see the Seattle skyline from the Seahawks' stadium.

Best Seat in the House

The Seahawks' stadium is
one of the loudest in the
world. The fans make sure
of that. They provide a boost
whenever the team needs it.
The stadium is also famous
for its wonderful views of
downtown Seattle.

SHOE BOX

The trading cards on these pages show some of the best Seahawks ever.

JIM ZORN

QUARTERBACK · 1976–1984

Jim had a strong arm and quick feet. He loved to scramble away from tacklers to throw touchdown passes.

STEVE LARGENT

RECEIVER · 1976–1989

Steve proved that NFL receivers don't need to be super fast. He caught a pass in 177 games in a row.

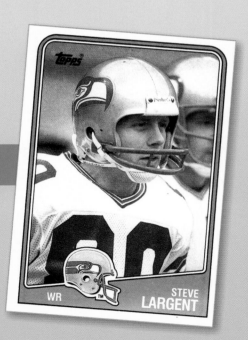

CORTEZ KENNEDY

DEFENSIVE TACKLE · 1990–2000

Cortez was very quick for a player his size. He made it almost impossible to run against the Seahawks.

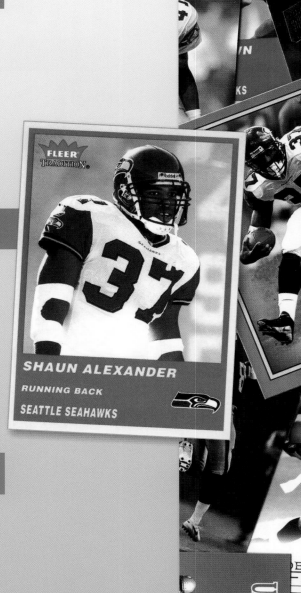

SHAUN ALEXANDER

RUNNING BACK · 2000–2007

Shaun had great balance and breakaway speed. He ran for more than 9,000 yards with the Seahawks.

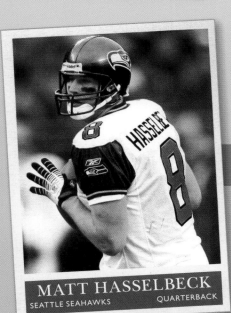

MATT HASSELBECK

QUARTERBACK · 2001–2010

Matt was a great leader. He guided the Seahawks to their first Super Bowl.

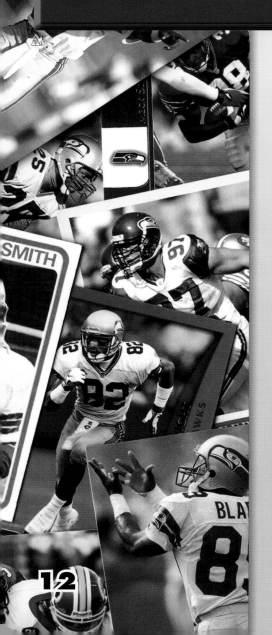

THE BIG PICTURE

Look at the two photos on page 13. Both appear to be the same. But they are not. There are three differences. Can you spot them?

Answers on page 23.

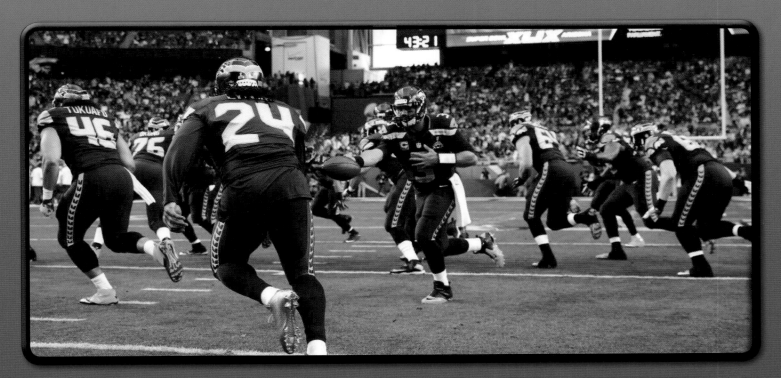

TRUE OR FALSE?

Russell Wilson was a star quarterback. Two of these facts about him are **TRUE**. One is **FALSE**. Do you know which is which?

1 Russell threw three touchdown passes in the **Pro Bowl** as a **rookie**.

2 Russell entertained his teammates by juggling bowling balls.

3 Russell ran for 849 yards and six touchdowns in 2014.

Answer on page 23.

Russell Wilson looks for an open receiver.

The Seahawks love having "The 12s" on their side.

Go Seahawks, Go!

Seahawks fans call themselves "The 12s." The players think of them as the twelfth player on the field. The Seahawks retired jersey #12 to honor their fans. A banner with that number flies above the field.

ON THE MAP

Here is a look at where five Seahawks were born, along with a fun fact about each.

 RICHARD SHERMAN · COMPTON, CALIFORNIA
Richard had 26 **interceptions** in his first five seasons.

 DAVE KRIEG · IOLA, WISCONSIN
Dave made the Pro Bowl three times for Seattle.

 WALTER JONES · ALICEVILLE, ALABAMA
Walter was an **All-Pro** four times for Seattle.

 EUGENE ROBINSON · HARTFORD, CONNECTICUT
Eugene led the NFL in interceptions in 1993.

 JON RYAN · REGINA, CANADA
Jon was the first punter to throw a touchdown pass in an NFL championship game.

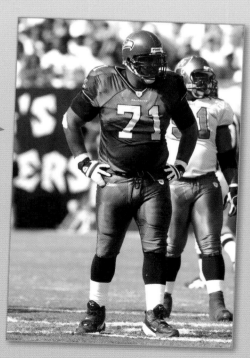

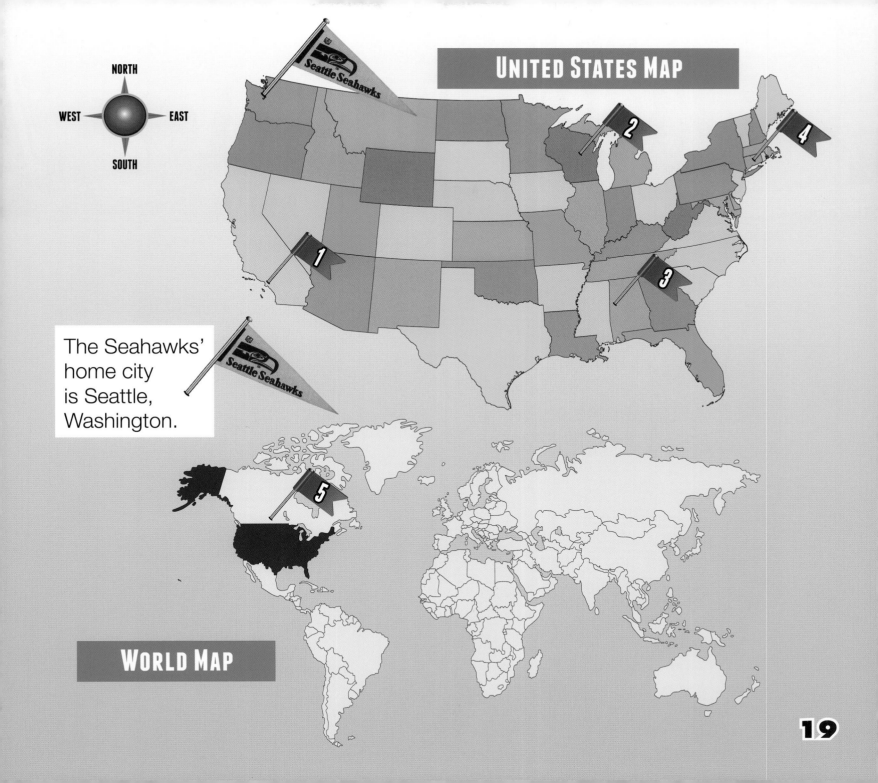

NORTH

WEST   EAST

SOUTH

UNITED STATES MAP

Seattle Seahawks

2

4

1

3

The Seahawks'
home city
is Seattle,
Washington.

Seattle Seahawks

5

WORLD MAP

19

Bobby Wagner wears the Seahawks' home uniform.

Football teams wear different uniforms for home and away games. The Seahawks' colors are blue and green. They also use white and neon green.

20

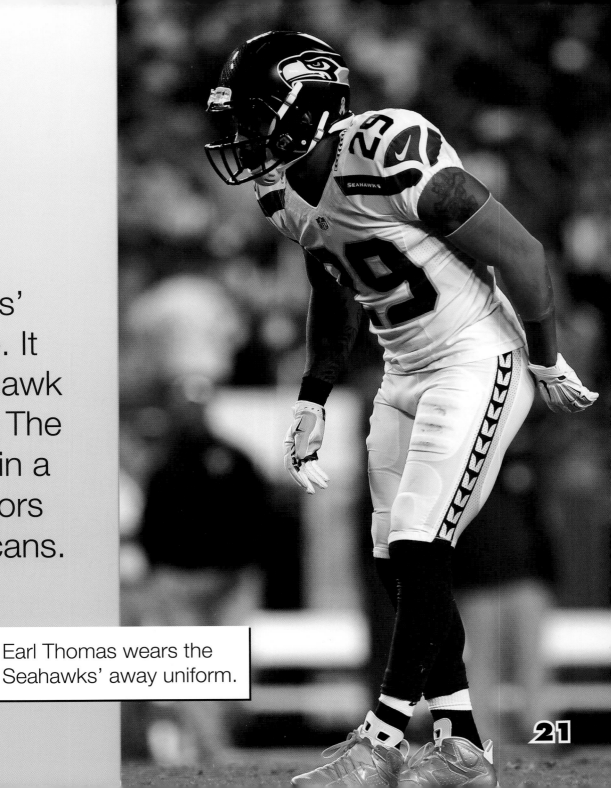

The Seahawks' helmet is blue. It shows a seahawk on each side. The bird is drawn in a style that honors Native Americans.

Earl Thomas wears the Seahawks' away uniform.

WE WON!

The Seahawks won their first Super Bowl at the end of the 2013 season. Coach Pete Carroll built his team around a strong defense. Linebacker **Malcolm Smith** was named the game's Most Valuable Player. He returned an interception 69 yards for a touchdown.

RECORD BOOK

These Seahawks set team records.

TOUCHDOWN PASSES	RECORD
Season: Russell Wilson (2015)	34
Career: **Dave Krieg**	195

TOUCHDOWN CATCHES	RECORD
Season: Doug Baldwin (2015)	14
Career: Steve Largent	100

RUSHING YARDS	RECORD
Season: Shaun Alexander (2005)	1,880
Career: Shaun Alexander	9,429

ANSWERS FOR THE BIG PICTURE
#24 changed to #54, the football changed to a basketball, and the time on the clock disappeared.

ANSWER FOR TRUE AND FALSE
#2 is false. Russell did not juggle bowling balls.

Football Words

All-Pro
An honor given to the best NFL player at each position.

Interceptions
Passes caught by a defensive player.

Pro Bowl
The NFL's annual all-star game.

Rookie
A player in his first season.

Index

Alexander, Shaun..................................11, **11**, 23
Baldwin, Doug..23
Carroll, Pete..22
Hasselbeck, Matt..11, **11**
Jones, Walter..18, **18**
Kennedy, Cortez..11, **11**
Krieg, Dave..18, 23, **23**
Largent, Steve..10, **10**, 23
Lynch, Marshawn..6, **6**
Robinson, Eugene..18
Ryan, Jon..18
Sherman, Richard..18
Smith, Malcolm..22, **22**
Thomas, Earl..**21**
Wagner, Bobby..**20**
Wilson, Russell......................6, **7**, 14, **15**, 23
Zorn, Jim..10, **10**

Photos are on **BOLD** numbered pages.

About the Author

Zack Burgess has been writing about sports for more than 20 years. He has lived all over the country and interviewed lots of All-Pro football players, including Brett Favre, Eddie George, Jerome Bettis, Shannon Sharpe, and Rich Gannon. Zack was the first African American beat writer to cover Major League Baseball when he worked for the *Kansas City Star*.

About the Seahawks

Learn more at these websites:

www.seahawks.com • www.profootballhof.com

www.teamspiritextras.com/Overtime/html/seahawks.html